BRIGLIN POTTERY
1948-1990

The Story of a Studio Pottery in the West End of London

by

Anthea Arnold

Foreword by Herbert Lom

BRIGLIN

1948- Impressed

HAND MADE BRIGLIN IN ENGLAND

BRIGLIN ENGLAND

1957- Printed    1957- Printed

Photographs by Josephine Appleby-Lom, Tony Clarke, Pauline Joyce and
from Briglin Archive

Print, design and reproduction by Flaydemouse, Yeovil, Somerset

Published by Briglin Books, 78 Bank Street, Maidstone, Kent ME14 1SJ

© Anthea Arnold 2002 ISBN 0 9541923 0 3

British Library Cataloguing-in-Publication Data. A catalogue record for
this book is available from the British Library

ACKNOWLEDGEMENTS

I would like to thank all the people who sent in the material which has gone to the making of this book. Obviously some contributed more than others, but it would be invidious to put them in an order of merit, so I will list them alphabetically. I have given the women the names they were using when they were involved with Briglin; where applicable, their present names are in brackets: Adrian Abberley, Barry Ball, Michael Black, Rosalind Bliss, Pam Butler (Jenkins), Tony Clarke, Julie Claydon (Villiers), Lyn Colavecchia (Lovitt), Frances Cooper (Benatt), Cathy Crawford, Michael Crosby-Jones, Lis Deane (Napier-Munn), George Dear, Alan Frewin, Tessa Fuchs, Laurel Hall, Martin Hardingham, John Houghton, Diane Ibanez, Chris Jenkins, Alan Peascod, Alan Pett, Kitty Roche, Rita Rummery, Stephen Russell, Graeme Storm, Guy Taplin, Sally Vinson, Alan Wallwork, Daphne Wells, Rosemary Wren, Cecily Wulff (Fisher), Max Zwissler. As well as providing material Lyn Lovitt and Sally Vinson have given me invaluable additional information and help. I would also like to thank Josephine, Brigitte's daughter and her husband Michael Bor, who have been unswervingly encouraging, generous and helpful; Mike Lovitt for all the help he has given me and Katrina Porteous, who read the typescript and gave me very valuable criticism. Most of all I would like to thank Brigitte's brother, Rainer. I could never have written the book without him. He has encouraged and supported me every step of the way and through it I have gained a very good friend.

AA

PREFACE

This book is very much Brigitte Appleby's. During 1999 she contacted many of the people who had been involved with Briglin over the years and asked them to write their memories. She wanted to make these into a book, which would include many illustrations and memorabilia of Briglin. She asked me if I would be interested in writing it up. My first reaction was to say 'no'; but then I read the material and talked more to Brigitte. Her enthusiasm was infectious. I said I would put up a proposal to her with no obligations on either side. I was anticipating an enterprise driven by the powerful motor of Brigitte with my role to apply the brakes and do a little manoeuvring.

Only a few days later she died.

I felt that the project had died with her; but her brother Rainer and her daughter Josephine were determined that it should go ahead. Sadly it lacks her memories, but I hope that she would have been fairly satisfied with the result. I hope too that it is enjoyable to read because over and over again the people who wrote about working at Briglin said that it was the most fruitful, the happiest time of their lives. What a tribute, which I know made her very proud and happy.

AA

CONTENTS

FOREWORD

I believe in the old song: *There is No Business Like Show Business*, but I would like to add: 'And there is nothing like the pottery business either'. The story of Briglin proves it. Both disciplines – acting and pottery making – are of course an art, a craft, a passion rather than a business. For years, once I was allowed into the workshop, there was nothing more fascinating for me than, for instance, catching Eileen whispering animatedly to a group of eager trainees about the magic of glazing (her whispering, as I call it, was part of her Englishness and modesty).

I remember looking forward to watching Brigitte throw a large pot with those firm Renaissance craftswoman's hands that could easily have inspired Michelangelo when he painted his great dramatic figures looking down from the Sistine Chapel. Although familiar with wearing costumes and make-up, I felt rather jealous of the young potters' 'exotic' (that is, dirty) appearance: filthy overalls, dripping fingers and smudgy noses; but I was also intrigued by the different clays, glazes and dangerous-looking high-voltage kilns. Brigitte, on the other hand, seemed enchanted by the extraordinary flamboyant artistry of the theatre world and, at the same time, the surprising ordinariness (for want of a better word) of some of the famous stage and screen stars, whom she met in the course of her and my work.

In the last scene of *The King and I*, in which I played the King of Siam (at the Theatre Royal, Drury Lane), the King dies of a broken heart, tragically, suddenly. The final curtain comes down a few minutes later. Brigitte died equally suddenly – not of a broken heart; the broken hearts are those of the people she left behind: our wonderful daughter Josephine, Brigitte's two brothers, myself and many, many others. She would not have liked final curtains coming down: 'Curtains are made for going up!' I hear her say, with that radiant smile: 'So tell everyone what fun it was and get on with it, darlings, do get on with it!'

Herbert Lom

CHAPTER I

STARTING OUT

In June 1948 Brigitte Goldsmith and Eileen Mawson – the Brig and Lin of Briglin – started a studio pottery in the basement of 66 Baker Street in the centre of London. Both were twenty-two years old. They had met at the Central School of Arts and Crafts and then worked for two years at Donald Mills Pottery in the Borough. London was pock-marked with bomb sites and rationing was still very much in place. The initial post-war euphoria over, the job of bringing life back to normal was gaining pace, helped by a hunger for anything that got away from the drab utilitarianism of the War years.

Brigitte and Eileen were very different in almost every way. Brigitte was tall, well-built with long, brown hair; Eileen was small, slight with short black hair. Brigitte was volcanically enthusiastic, emotional and noisy; Eileen was careful, calm and quite quiet. Brigitte of course, was the one you noticed, but without Eileen the business would never have survived. She had the ability to listen and then quietly summarise what the more vociferous Brigitte and others had said. They complemented each other ideally, their differences produced a creative dynamic and both had an enormous capacity for work.

They came from very different backgrounds. Brigitte was born in Leipzig on September 13, 1926 of German Jewish parents. Her father was a furrier, her mother a doctor. When Hitler began to threaten the Jews they moved from Germany to England, to a large house in Surrey. She went to Guildford High School and her first ambition was to be a nurse. However, the headmistress refused to give her a reference, saying that she never stuck to anything for any length of time and nursing would not be a suitable career. Influenced by her aunt, Hilde Goldschmidt, an artist in the German Expressionist School, she went instead to the Central School of Arts and Crafts. Although she started by studying painting, pottery soon took over. She loved everything about it: the feel of the clay, the physical activity, the open-endedness, the creating of something beautiful out of something so unprepossessing. As a result of the War, the pottery department was very run-down, but, undaunted, Brigitte caused a course to be created just for her.

Eileen was born in 1925 in Streatham, a suburb of London. In 1941 she went to the West of England School of Art in Bristol to study painting and in 1943 continued her painting studies at Beckenham School of Art. She then went on to take a teacher training course at the Institute of Education in London where she was introduced to pottery for the first time. The classes were taken at the nearby Central School of Arts and Crafts where she was taught by Gilbert Harding-Green and his assistant Donald Mills. It was Donald Mills who inspired her love of pottery. In her last term at the College he recommended that she read Bernard Leach's *A Potter's Book,* which cemented her desire to become a potter. In 1945 she got a job teaching art at Derby School of Art where she was taught by R.J. Washington who furthered her enthusiasm for clay and firing. A year later, in 1946, she moved back to London to join Donald Mills' studio.

He had been a student at the Central School of Arts and Crafts and then became a technical assistant. After a spell at the Leach Pottery in St Ives and then the Fulham Pottery in London – a factory pottery where he was expected to throw a hundred and twenty pots a day – he decided, in 1945, that he wanted to start his own workshop. He found premises just south of London Bridge near to St George's Church, which had been badly bombed. The building itself was bomb-damaged, but he rebuilt walls, put in windows and made himself a couple of treadle wheels. He then acquired a gas kiln and the first firings took place in February 1946. By this time he had been joined by three others, who had been students at the Central School of Arts and Crafts – two of whom were Brigitte and Eileen.

By the end of 1946 there were five partners working together, sharing the throwing, firing, packing, distributing and also producing their own individual pots. The aim was to produce five hundred pots a week, which were all pre-ordered. These large orders were for stoneware, which he had learned to work with under Bernard Leach in St Ives. The pottery, under the influence of Ted Baker, who had joined them in December 1946, was also experimenting with earthenware: new, artistic shapes, new glazes and free decoration, all of which was a break from the plain, solid stoneware. It was this experience and the influence of Dora Billington, one of their teachers at the Central School, which was later to be seen in the work of the Briglin potters.

Alongside these two lines they were turning out electrical refractories – the elements used in electric fires – and at one time the whole pottery was producing nothing else. However, this line was ultimately to be its downfall. They were given an order for 250,000 elements, which were made but never paid for. As a result in 1948 the firm went bankrupt and the partners divided what was left between them. Brigitte and Eileen acquired a kiln.

Life is full of chance meetings, none more so than Brigitte's meeting with the actor, Herbert Lom, which was to have a lasting impact on her life. Two psychiatrists –

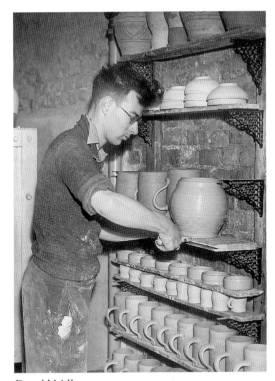

Donald Mills.

Experimental earthenware.

Dr George Morgan and his wife Dr Elizabeth Tylden – had a practice close-by Donald Mills in the Borough and had asked him if they could send patients to the pottery for occupational rehabilitation. A number of patients came regularly to do routine jobs and were paid a minimal wage. One day Brigitte was supervising a woman who was weeping inconsolably and asking for her baby. She was the first wife of Walter Bor, a friend of Herbert Lom. It was at a weekly gathering at the doctors' house that Brigitte first met Herbert, which was to be the start of a life-long, if not continuous, involvement with him. Even more coincidentally, the baby the patient was crying for – Michael Bor – is now married to Brigitte and Herbert's daughter Josephine. But all that was much later.

Brigitte was living in a flat at 67 George Street. Just round the corner, at 66 Baker Street, was a disused basement stretching back about a hundred feet. In April 1948 they signed a ten year lease on it and on June 24 secured a Memorandum and Articles of Association for Briglin Pottery Limited. In those days Baker Street consisted of Georgian terraces, broken only by bomb sites. Neglect had turned the yellow London brick black; the entrance and the stairs of No. 66 were dark and dingy. With the help of £400 capital, given to Brigitte by her father, they cleared, rebuilt, painted and equipped the basement. A packing room at the front led into an office and at the back was the pottery itself, with the kiln and one wheel. Their first firing consisted of blue and white majolica mugs and one cup and saucer, which were shown to the buyers from Heals and Selfridges. The solitary cup and saucer resulted in an order from Selfridges for a dozen teasets. Briglin was on its way. At first it proceeded slightly haltingly, as they found it difficult to throw cups that were the same size and shape; but that soon passed and orders kept coming. By the autumn they were exhausted. Brigitte set off for the Lake District and Eileen for Brighton. However, when they got there both spent their time going round shops looking for orders, rather than taking a holiday.

The aim from the start was to produce useful but decorative domestic earthenware and to sell it at a reasonable price. Rather like William Morris and the Bloomsbury Group before them, the Briglin potters were breaking away from the present fashion – which reflected the past – and turning to other influences. The effect of Bernard Leach was powerful and most contemporary potters felt that to break away from the rugged stoneware, that he had made so fashionable, would be impossible. The only decorated pottery was factory-made and was all sent for export. The white Briglin earthenware, with its tin glaze and oxide decoration, was much nearer to Scandinavian ware than most of the things that were being produced in England at the time. By the spring of 1949 orders were coming in steadily and they were employing one person to share the work. She was a school leaver called Janice, who was learning to wedge clay, pull and put on handles and mix glaze and slips.

One afternoon in April 1949 Daphne Wells walked down the steep stairs to the basement. She was looking for work. She had eighteen months' experience: six months decorating at Gustavsberg Ceramic Factory in Sweden, six months throwing in the studio of Reginald Lewis at Coleshill, Birmingham and six months with Donald Mills, who had re-started his pottery in South London. She had learnt a lot about production-throwing and discipline from him, but had found him a hard and authoritarian task-master; he had not paid a living wage and had not encouraged her in any way. She had heard from him many disparaging remarks about these two women, who were too inexperienced, frivolous and foolish to set up on their own. Coming from him, this sounded to her like a good recommendation for the sort of place she wanted to work in.

At the time she arrived Brigitte was ill with hepatitis and Eileen was struggling to keep up with the orders. She took Daphne on for three weeks, which was to be the start of six years with Briglin and the start of the expansion of the pottery to include many other apprentice and more experienced potters.

Recently Daphne described what working at 66 Baker Street was like: "The studio operated as a close-knit workshop, everyone collaborating in the stages of production. The routine was divided but there was always room for flexibility and improvisation. Eileen laid out the orders; a young apprentice looked after the clay and supplied it prepared and weighed for throwing; Brigitte and I threw and trimmed; an apprentice sponged rims and stacked for drying; handles and slip work were done by Janice; glazing and kiln-work by Eileen; Brigitte and Eileen decorated; lesser skilled workers made model animals from press moulds; Eileen did invoicing and book-keeping; Brigitte looked after buyers and sales and promotion. We all cleaned up, the floor was

The first teacups.

kept dust free with daily vacuuming and 'who's turn to make the coffee?' was the cry about 10.30 every morning. We also took turns packing the finished orders in tea chests for shipment by Carter Patterson, until Mr Houghton took it over. He arrived at the end of the afternoon after his day job and worked late into the evening. He was a wonderful cheerful Cockney, who regaled us with endless jokes, anecdotes and teasing. He stayed with Briglin until it closed in 1990, when he was eighty-one years old.

"Clay arrived by lorry from Stoke on Trent – two tons at a time – covered with canvas tarpaulins. The rolls of clay from the industrial pug were about three feet long and four to six inches in diameter, heavy, awkward and often wet and sticky if they had been rained on during their overnight journey. When the lorry drew up to the kerb in front of 66, all hands were recruited: one person was on the lorry handing down the clay to others, who lowered it through an old coal-hole in the pavement to the cellar below. From there it was carried about a hundred feet into the studio, stacked in the 'clay cupboard' and covered with sacking, towels and tarpaulin. This long, narrow space – and indeed the whole basement – smelt of damp and mould and clay from the daily spraying with water, which was needed to keep the clay in good condition.

"Although a basement studio, the workshop was light and bright and spacious, painted in attractive colours. The wheel was a stand-up electric 'Britannia' made by Fulham Road Pottery Works and had a brass ejector head to hold plaster bats and a foot pedal for speed control. Commercially prepared white earthenware clay was used and either decorated with light or dark blue slip, with sgraffitto line decoration and finished with transparent glaze; or glazed white and decorated with simple overglaze brush decoration. It was fired in an electric kiln (Catterson Smith to 1120°C).

"I was given every encouragement to contribute new shapes and experiment with design – I made the first teapot and Brigitte had a passport photo taken of it. I was in potter's heaven! New goals for production were continually being met and surpassed and it became possible to raise wages to a good living standard. It was an exciting team effort. Throughout my years at Briglin encouragement and enthusiasm were always the prevailing atmosphere. Along with all the work we had a lot of fun and socialising. Jokes and recipes were brought each day to be shared. Favourite dishes and gourmet discoveries were tasted and criticised. Friends and relatives dropped in to visit. But conversation never interrupted the work routine".

The speed with which Briglin Pottery gained popularity and recognition was partly due to the bright, colourful designs and its practical, serviceable nature; but it was also due to Brigitte's energy and enthusiasm in introducing it to buyers and giving it publicity through the trade press. It was sometimes said that she could sell anything to anybody; this was unfair, as she would not have tried to sell something that she did not

At work in Baker Street.

Passport photo of the first teapot.

believe in. But, if she did believe in it, she could sell it. Many potters and artists are diffident about selling and getting publicity. She was not. In 1949 this small basement pottery was written up in the *Pottery Gazette and Glass Trade Review* and in 1951 a selection of its pots were exhibited at the Festival of Britain.

In 1950 Brigitte married Stephen Appleby and two years later Eileen married Oscar Lewenstein. They both continued to work as hard as ever. Brigitte had acquired a 1928 London taxi, which she called Nellie; often at weekends the Briglin 'family' would go on outings to country potters, to the sea-side, to her parents' house in Effingham, to Kent to pick cherries. When the weather was hot, lunch-hours were extended to two hours, so that they could swim in the Serpentine in Hyde Park. The extra hour was made up by starting an hour earlier in the morning. Alternatively, they would swim at six o'clock in the morning, have a kipper breakfast at the Marble Arch, Lyons Corner House and then start work as usual.

By this time they were turning out about four hundred pieces a week, all of which had been pre-ordered and included a number for the USA. In addition to the mugs, coffee and tea-sets, jugs, bowls and other standard lines, they specialized in

Festival of Britain Certificate.

commemorative pieces for weddings, birthdays and other occasions, which included customer's names and dates in the design. One of the first mugs they ever made was for Prince Charles. It seems that an old acquaintance of theirs was a personal friend of Princess Elizabeth and had told her of the two young women potters who had started a pottery in what had been the kitchen quarters in a basement in Baker Street. She had obviously remembered this story and when Prince Charles was born they received a letter from Buckingham Palace asking them to make a mug with his name and date of birth engraved on it. Two years later they made a similar one for Princess Anne. In 1957, Briglin made mugs for each member of the Trans Antarctic expedition, which included Brigitte's brother Rainer.

This busy, happy way of living and working continued until one night late in 1952. A fire, caused by an electrical fault, had started in the packing room and rapidly spread through the basement and up the well of the building. The following morning insurance assessors, landlords and leasehold representatives, including one from the Crown Commissioners, were lined up on the pavement outside. A wet, burnt smell hung over everything. The packing room was awash with black water, the office had been gutted and the pottery was a mass of broken, charred pots. Only the kilns remained undamaged.

For a short time it seemed that the story was over. But the War had taught people to put up with hardship, to be stoical and optimistic. Soon the rubble had been shovelled out of the basement and what was left was almost exactly the same as when they first saw it in 1948. They thrived on challenges. This time they could afford to have an architect and, having learnt from their experience of working there, could redesign it to make far better use of the space. The thing Brigitte really craved was a showroom, where the Briglin pots could be displayed and where buyers could come and see them.

An architect, Douglas Stephen, was hired to design it. He was a friend and an enthusiastic buyer of their pottery. Scaffolding was put up and the building work got under way. Surrounded by scaffolding and builders, the work of producing pots and filling orders soon resumed.

CHAPTER 2

STARTING AGAIN

The rebuilt pottery was officially opened with a party on December 10, 1953. Daphne described the newly designed basement: "When the remodelling was finished and the bright new painting completed, there was a wonderful, new, beautiful showroom in place of the old packing room, in which to display the full range of Briglin pottery. The showroom was a thoroughly modern affair and included a smart office. The old office was now a new throwing and trimming area, with two wheels backed against a coral pink wall, decorated with small white stars. All the trim was painted white as were a bank of new wooden, pot-racks. We had all been inspired to create many exhibition pieces for the grand opening and they looked good spotlighted and displayed on the glass shelving in the showroom. The attendance at the opening was impressive, with many public figures and representatives from trade journals and magazines. From a potter's perspective it was a major social event".

Amongst the guests were members of the cast of *The King and I* which had just opened at Drury Lane. Herbert Lom was playing the lead and had shaved his head for the part. His leading lady was Valerie Hobson. They certainly added glamour to the occasion and the Briglin potters had made seventy five special mugs, one for each member of the cast and the orchestra.

The new Briglin Pottery was written up in a number of journals. *The Pottery Gazette and Glass Trade Review* in its February 1954 issue said: "In December last year a very modern showroom was opened. Designed by Douglas Stephen & Partners, it demonstrates dramatically what can be done with one small room. The walls are an almost startling white, in contrast to the lime green ceiling, and one sliding-door panel of a large built-in fitment, opposite the entrance to the showroom, is painted a bright scarlet, to create further interest. Apart from the vivid splashes of colour everything else is subordinated to the ware on show... A very modern and effective little showroom, all the more surprising because it is situated in a basement in Baker Street". *The Pottery Gazette and Glass Trade Review* said of them in the January 1954 issue: "Here at Briglin Pottery is good workmanship and that new liveliness in design that one looks for in vain amongst some of the old-established pottery manufacturers. The Briglin potters know what is happening in the contemporary world, and their earthenware proclaims the fact".

STARTING AGAIN

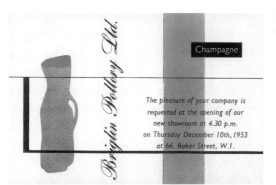

Invitation to the
Opening Party.

The new showroom.

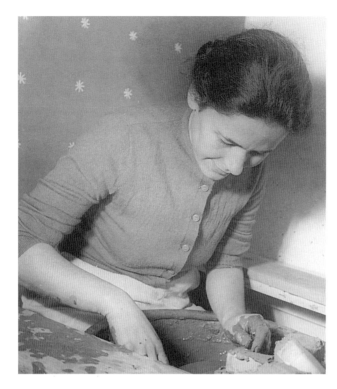

Brigitte Appleby.

Eileen Lewenstein.

Daphne Wells.

One of the first long runs, after the opening of the new pottery, was of Coronation ashtrays. These four inch shallow dishes were stamped with the commemorative Coronation design and glazed in six bright colours. The stamp was carved by Eileen and then a series of them were cast in plaster. Daphne recalls: "Brigitte and I would sometimes sit for days of intensive sessions completing large orders, such as Coronation ashtrays. With this repetitive work the time sped by with games of beating our own record each day, sharing the books we were reading, taking trips of the imagination, such as an African Safari and, as always, sharing new recipes". This Coronation Souvenir was given the Council of Industrial Design Certificate in 1953.

Soon more members were introduced into the team. At one time there were as many as ten – some of them part-timers. These included Tony Barson and Fred Millett both of whom were artists who decorated special plates, bowls and mugs. Tony Barson decorated commemorative pieces, specializing in plates showing a picture of the church that couples got married in. He also painted humorous, cartoon-like characters with beautiful lettering on mugs and plates. One of the team, Pat Birks, described him as "Dear Tony Barson, who used to entertain us as we were working, with his re-telling of the plot and much of the dialogue of the film he had seen that week. Better than the radio, any time."

Some who joined the team were totally inexperienced, often straight out of art school; others had some experience. Many spent a period with Briglin and then left to set up their own potteries. All remembered their days at Briglin as exciting, educational and very hard work. George Dear expressed the sentiments of many when he wrote recently, "Brigitte and Eileen and all the many friends I made at Briglin have

Coronation Ashtray.

THE CORONATION OF HER MAJESTY QUEEN ELIZABETH II

Design Review of Coronation Souvenirs

This certifies acceptance by The Council of Industrial Design of
the Coronation pottery
approved by the Coronation Souvenirs Committee and included
in Design Review

submitted by
Briglin Pottery Limited

CERTIFICATE No. 24   FOR THE COUNCIL OF INDUSTRIAL DESIGN   DATE 1.1.1953

Articles thus accepted may be marked 'Coronation Souvenir approved by the Council of Industrial Design' and a card with these words, may be displayed with them

Bowls, plates and mug by Tony Barson.

Plates by Fred Miller.

been my constant all these years in an otherwise random universe. Brigitte and associates have become lifelong friends. I count myself very fortunate to have spent my formative years in such a positive caring 'clan' and I have used the skills learned at Briglin to good effect to this very day".

When George came to the pottery in 1954 he was fifteen. As he walked down the steep stairs to what others often described as the Dickensian basement, he was almost certainly nervous, but probably did not notice his surroundings. He came from a truly Dickensian place. Because of a very difficult home life, he had been sent to live in an institution called The Royal Philanthropic Society, which he describes as 'a Victorian home for waifs and strays'. The regime was strict and tough, the only redeeming feature being a fully equipped pottery, run like the Leach pottery in St Ives. In charge was a Mr Garlic, a very small man, with thick glasses, a boxer dog almost as large as he was and a full strength Capstan cigarette always hanging from his lips. His real job was head of English, but he rushed round filling many other roles as well. When George was fourteen he was chosen by Mr Garlic to be his assistant in the pottery. He was trained to throw and do all the other basic things necessary to produce a simple pot. It was Mr Garlic who approached Briglin Pottery, in an effort to place George as an apprentice. He drove him to the pottery to be interviewed. Brigitte remembered discussing glazes with him. They were having trouble with their white glaze crazing. He told them to use a Wenger's tin glaze, which they did without any further trouble for many years.

George lived twelve miles away in a room in North London and cycled to Baker Street and back every morning and evening. To begin with he did all the menial jobs: weighing clay for the throwers, fetching, carrying, tidying up, making coffee. When free of these duties he was allowed to throw and turn. He started with the simple shapes he had been taught by Mr Garlic but gradually became more proficient. He remembers, "we all worked extremely hard making mugs, slipped sgraffittoed ashtrays, flower pots and saucers, pig and hedgehog money boxes. We were expected to make so many an hour, there were always targets, production schedules and quality standards were high".

The decorated flower pots and saucers were a relatively new line using red clay. The rims of the pots were white glazed, the lower part remaining undecorated and unglazed. Decorations in combinations of yellow, turquoise, green, blue, black and white were painted on top of the glaze and fired rim to rim, one inside the other. They ranged from ten inches in diameter down to three and were stacked in the kiln with no shelving. One of the constant aims at Briglin was to save time and kiln space. Later, when Pat Birks left the team to set up on her own, she took the making of the flower pots with her.

Ashtrays with sgraffito decoration.

Pig money boxes.

Flower pots.

The range and variety of lines increased enormously between the end of 1953 and 1955 and set the pattern of pots to be made by Briglin for some years to come. Although most of the pots continued to be made of white clay a certain amount of red clay was introduced. The simple, over-glazed, majolica method of decoration was still extensively used and the wax-resist technique was introduced and used more and more over the succeeding years. Among the standard lines produced at this time the illustrations show a fifteen piece wax resist coffee set, grey on white; wax resist pint sized cups and saucers; a black and white coffee set with extruded handles, painted thickly with manganese oxide, then white glazed inside and around the top – this design showed the influence of Lucie Rie, a lifelong friend of Brigitte's. Other standard lines were Guernsey jugs in various sizes with a feather decoration in black or light blue; covered butter dishes decorated dark blue on white; half a dozen spice jars in blue, black or green with herbs or spices inside and their names on the outside; salt and pepper sets and the ever popular named mugs. The illustrated sherry set – a decanter in the shape of a stolid porker and six tumblers – was made of red clay and introduced the *scroll* decoration, which was later to become one of the standard Briglin designs. There were also plates – some special, orders with names and places painted on by the artists – ashtrays, bowls, vases and animals of all kinds.

Brigitte and Eileen always encouraged all the members of the team to contribute ideas for new shapes and designs. As many of the potters were, like George, young and

Coffee set – unglazed managaneze oxide with white glazed rim.

Wax resist coffee set.

Wax resist cups and saucers.

Porker sherry set with *Scroll* decoration.

George Dear surrounded by pots in the showroom.

inexperienced, they would often stay on after the pottery closed in the evening to try out ideas of their own. In order to encourage them to do this, it was decided that Thursday afternoons – unless there was a real rush on – should be set aside for the making of individual pots. So successful was this that Heals staged an exhibition of pots made outside the Briglin range by George, Eileen and Brigitte.

Selfridges and Heals continued to be the main outlets, but the range of shops was gradually widened by Brigitte's energetic selling and promoting. Joshua Taylor, a family-run department store in Cambridge, was amongst the new and successful outlets. An area on the ground floor was transformed into a pottery gallery, showing a variety of modern domestic items, including a large number from Briglin. Briglin pots were shown and promoted at exhibitions and demonstrations round the country and written up in House and Garden and Vogue as well as in the trade press. One of the most memorable of these demonstrations was at the International Handicrafts Exhibition at Olympia in 1956. It was opened by Clement Attlee, by that time Earl Attlee. He declined to try his hand at the wheel but watched intently as Brigitte turned a two pint tankard. She said she would send it to him when it was fired. "I'm afraid I don't drink beer," he said, "I shall stick flowers in it". Brigitte managed to get a facsimile of Earl Attlee's signature, reproduced from the Berlin Conference of 1945, copied it onto the tankard and sent it to him.

Bowl out of the standard Briglin range.

More pots out of the standard Briglin range.

Earl Attlee at the International Handicrafts Exhibition.

In 1955 Daphne left to set up her own studio. When Tessa Fuchs joined the team in 1956, both Brigitte and Eileen were heavily pregnant. Brigitte's marriage to Stephen Appleby did not last long. After eighteen months they had separated and she had resumed her relationship with Herbert Lom. He had recently made *The Lady Killers* and played Napoleon in King Vidor's *War and Peace*. Their daughter Josephine was born on December 18, 1956. Brigitte never worried about flouting convention, in fact she rather enjoyed it, and the birth of her daughter was a very joyous event. She almost immediately moved into a larger flat in Hyde Park Square, where she could have someone living in to look after her daughter and allow her to continue to work. As well as a number of nannies and later au pair girls, Brigitte's mother was always there to give help and support when it was needed.

Coincidentally, Eileen was also involved with the theatre through her husband Oscar, who had run Unity Theatre in London and Glasgow and in 1952 had become Artistic Director of the Royal Court Theatre Club in London. Over the years this theatrical involvement was to have a considerable influence on Briglin, both in the people associated with it and the pots that were made. In the early days of Baker Street, one visitor walked down the dingy stairs to the basement and was amazed to find herself face to face with Ginger Rogers. Herbert Lom had brought her to the pottery to ask Brigitte and Eileen if they would teach her boyfriend – a French actor – how to throw a pot, which he had to do in the film that he was making at the time. This was the first of a number of such requests.

In 1956 Briglin was added to the Design Index and their pottery was displayed at the Design Centre in the Haymarket and included in their travelling exhibitions. The Design Centre had been established as a direct result of the 1951 Festival of Britain to approve and promote good design in Britain. The great advantage of being included in the Index was that it opened the way to exporting to other countries. In 1957 Briglin expanded its exports to the USA. A year later Chris Jenkins recalls, they had "an order for trillions of mugs for Nieman Marcus, which I always think of when I hear people talking of studio pottery". Over the years the volume of exports grew steadily and by 1969 approximately twenty percent of the production was going overseas to the USA, Sweden, Denmark, Australia, New Zealand, Canada, Japan, Italy, South America, the Bahamas, New Guinea and others.

1958 was a year of great change at Briglin. In 1956 Eileen had a second son, Peter – the first, Mark, had been born in1953 – and when he was two years old, decided that she could no longer devote enough time to the pottery. She resigned, leaving Brigitte as the sole partner. The ten year lease on 66 Baker Street ran out that year and Brigitte decided not to renew it but to look for larger premises. Just round the corner from Baker Street she found a property with a sizeable ground floor area, which could be used as a showroom and shop, and a basement, that could be converted into a pottery and packing area. She signed the lease on 22 Crawford Street.

The very first animals.

CHAPTER 3

22 CRAWFORD STREET

Eileen had always been the cautious, careful one, essential in the early stages of setting up the business, but now Brigitte wanted to branch out and especially to be able to sell direct to the public – to have a shop. She was above all a potter, but she was much, much more. At Crawford Street she created a unique training ground for aspiring potters – at one time she had as many as fourteen people working in the basement – she brought out their talents, encouraged them, made them feel good, but insisted on high standards and very, very hard work, which she rewarded with praise and lots of fun. Working for Briglin, when Brigitte was in charge, was a unique experience. No day was quite the same as the one before. The only thing that was constant was the massive amount of work produced.

Mike Crosby-Jones, who worked there from 1966 to 1971, recently wrote: "There was a time when Briglin was seen as one of the most, if not *the* most, important training workshop for fast and good throwing. The form was mainly the straight cylinder, which is the foundation of good design. The material finish, the very sophisticated use of hot wax, the firing of earthenware at temperatures normally associated with stoneware, the colours of manganese, cobalt and copper, all made for a very distinctive and comprehensive range of tableware at ordinary prices. Also, to Briglin's credit, everyone who worked there was paid. There were never 'paying' students and there could well have been". The time that he was writing about was when Briglin was at the height of its influence and productivity, producing over three thousand pieces a week.

It was a fairly unique place for customers too. Tony Barson told of an exhibition of his paintings in the shop. The front of the shop had been turned into a gallery, there was a bowl of punch, Briglin goblets to drink it out of and lots of things to eat. The time for the exhibition to open arrived, but there was no sign of Brigitte. A number of people came in. Tony, who at the best of times could hardly bear to sell anything to anybody, did not make himself known. There was a general feeling of 'why are we here?' Then Brigitte arrived. She was in no way an aggressive sales person, but she managed to create an atmosphere of enthusiasm, which made people want to do things, including buying pots and pictures. Within a very short time almost all the pictures were sold and everyone was enjoying themselves.

A similar atmosphere was created in the shop every Friday evening. Work stopped at five o'clock and the workers would come up from the basement, still covered in clay, to unwind with food and drink provided by Brigitte. Unsuspecting customers would sometimes be involved in this too. Overwhelmed by the hospitality, they would not be quite sure what was going on, not quite sure whether they should be there or not; but soon, most were enjoying a most unusual shopping experience.

That was how Crawford Street developed over the years. The move from Baker Street took place on a Saturday morning. Brigitte had hired the architect Bill Siddons to transform the ground floor into a gallery and shop. To this day the layout is much as it was then. Sally Vinson remembers that a mobile crane had been hired to lift the kilns through the pavement hatches in Baker Street, on to a lorry, which drove slowly round the corner to Crawford Street, where they were lowered through similar hatches to the basement. Work stopped at Baker Street on Friday evening and started again in Crawford Street the following Monday morning.

Although Briglin was essentially modern and commercial, Brigitte had a great interest in, and respect for, traditional pottery. Before she left Baker Street she had, with the help of Herbert Lom, set in motion a project to revive an old Staffordshire tradition of producing figurines of famous people. She had contacted Richard and Susan Parkinson and discussed the possibility of producing a hundred pieces of seven theatrical personalities: Vivien Leigh as Cleopatra, Dame Margot Fonteyn as Ondine, Sir John Gielgud as Hamlet, Sir Laurence Olivier as Henry V, Paul Robeson as

Crane lowering a kiln into 22 Crawford Street.

Figurines of Paul Robeson as Othello and Laurence Olivier as Henry V.

Brigitte with Vivien Leigh and the figurines of her and Laurence Olivier.

Othello, Maria Callas as Violetta and Sir Alec Guinness as himself. Herbert Lom went personally to get permission from each of them, which was readily given; he also wrote and signed a publicity leaflet. In the end only the first five were made. The figurines, devised by Richard Parkinson, were ten inches high, slip cast from continental-type hard paste porcelain, which has to be fired at extremely high temperatures. The wastage was about fifty percent. The only colours that were used in decoration were green and black. The five figures were displayed at the Design Centre in 1959, where they were seen by the Duke of Edinburgh, who bought a set, as did Charlton Heston. Brigitte went to Vivien Leigh's dressing room at the New Theatre to present her with the figures of herself and her husband, Laurence Olivier. For a while Briglin was as well known for the figurines as for its own pots. Originally priced at ten guineas each, or forty guineas for the set, they have since become collectors' pieces, changing hands for a considerably higher price than that.

At the party to mark the opening of 22 Crawford Street on May 8, 1959 Brigitte had the novel idea of inviting the guests to make their own pots. The actor Peter Sellers was amongst them. A journalist at the time wrote, "With a twist of his mouth and a flick of his eyebrows he bounced to a seat at the wheel. He caressed the untried clay, gingerly plucked at the wheel with his big toe. Some time later a strange sight

Peter Sellers decorating Goon figures.

arose. This was no normal jug or cup or plate, this was six inches of bell-shaped Arch-Type Goon with unruly, stick-out hair and a primitive club, swung nonchalantly over one shoulder. Peter chuckled. Into the oven he popped his Goon and baked it. Arch-Type emerged to be hand-painted in white with coke black hair, dot crossed eyes and coloured patches – essentially part of a proper Arch-Goon. Delighted, he departed with the Goon under one arm, leaving a new-born idea behind him". This, of course, was not what really happened. Chris Jenkins remembers teaching Peter Sellers – not very successfully – to throw a pot and later rescuing a soggy cone to make a Goon with club and spiky hair, which was fired and subsequently decorated by Peter Sellers. He later drew sketches of other characters from which Goon figures were produced and sold in large numbers.

The idea of allowing people from outside to try their hand at potting continued. Rosalind Bliss remembers an old lady, who used to come in regularly to create rather misshapen animals, which were later improved, glazed and fired ready to be collected by their proud creator.

Although 22 Crawford Street with its well designed spacious shop, was far more welcoming than 66 Baker Street, the studio was still in the basement. Lyn Colavecchia, who joined the team in 1963, gives a very vivid picture of the layout and what it was like to work there:

"You went down creaking wooden stairs to the basement. Every inch of space was used – divided and sub-divided into specific working areas. "Furthest from the stairs was the throwing and turning room, which housed four electric wheels and the racking and storage space for work in progress. A frosted-glass roof-light shed a small amount of daylight, allowing a filtered impression of the weather outside. It shone brightly on sunny days, dulling to a grey rectangle on gloomy days or as evening fell. In wet weather raindrops drummed loudly against the glass.

"At the end of this room, and open to it, lay the area known as the decorating room, which also meant the glazing room, the putting-on-handles room and the tea-making room. The decorating table was large enough for two people to sit side by side, with a board of work to decorate beside them. Wax resist and oxides were used on both raw and biscuited pots. A container of candle wax, mixed with paraffin, was kept hot all day long, while patterns known as *scroll, willow* and *daisy* were painted with manganese oxide on to mugs, jugs, coffee pots; raw cylinders, vases and lamp-bases were freely decorated with scratched and gouged sgraffitto.

"Glazing was carried out on a little table set at right angles to the decorating table. A large dustbin of Wenger's white glaze was mixed regularly and was used on all the pots. It was a wonderfully stable high-firing earthenware glaze, which allowed oxides

Turning and decorating.

to show through with just the right intensity, with the colour of the red clay giving a warm, toasted look. So cosily intimate was this little working area that one could turn from glazing to the sink in one movement, put the kettle on, make the tea and turn back to decorate more pots. On sunny days we would often troop upstairs to sit on the steps of the pottery and watch the passers-by watching us.

"Through a doorway, directly beside the sink, lay the foot of the stairs and a few shelves. This was where Rosalind Bliss worked as quality controller. She was so conscientious a controller and the criteria by which she measured the quality of the pots so demanding that her pile of seconds had often to be secretly reinstated as firsts by Mr Houghton, to pack into his wood-wool packed tea chests. Two evenings a week, while the rest of the pottery lay quiet and in darkness, Mr Houghton could be seen in his theatrically-lit packing space, surrounded by pots, paper, woodshavings and tea chests, with only the sound of his little tinny radio to keep him company. Five, six, seven packing cases would be filled each week and carried up the stairs to be collected by British Road Service vans and delivered around the country and for export.

"Beyond this little area, directly under the front half of the shop, was the kiln room, with its three kilns: two Studio 5A Chromartie and the original, small Catterson Smith, which was used for biscuit firing. The kilns were hardly ever allowed to get completely cold. We cooled them down as quickly as possible to 400°C, unpacked them with gloves and towels in order to pack them once more with pots and get them turned on again before lunchtime and before they got below 200°C. We would fling open the glass-blocked pavement hatches to allow the heat and the burning-off wax fumes to escape into the street. We underground workers would gain a glimpse of the sky and the legs of pedestrians, while they, in turn, could peer down on to the wedging and weighing-up bench below and, during the winter, warm themselves with the up-draught of escaping heat".

Larger pots and plates showing a variety of techniques.

Beyond the kilns, under the pavement, was a tunnel where the clay was stored. Five tons at a time would be delivered every two months by lorry from Mellors in Stoke-on- Trent. As in Baker Street, this would be man-handled from the lorry, through the glass-blocked pavement hatches into the basement. By the mid Sixties, they were using nothing but a red earthenware clay, which had a very fine grog in it that helped fast throwing, drying and turning. In this area too was the Bolton pug machine that whirred away unceasingly all day.

In the Sixties the throwing and turning was done by a team of six, which included John Virando, Alan Pett, Mike Crosby-Jones and for a while Alan Frewin. The wheels used were a Taylor and a Burton. Although the main throwing and turning was done by a core of skilled people, everyone, as Lyn Colavecchia remembers, "was encouraged to throw and try out ideas if they wanted to and often Brigitte would sit at the wheel, her tongue protruding between her firmly closed lips, clay smeared at random over her face and clothes, throwing the little miniatures she loved to make and trying out new designs". Everything was designed on the wheel, never on paper. The freedom to experiment, to try out new talents was very much a part of the Briglin ethos and marks the difference between a co-operative enterprise and a production line.

Lyn demonstrates this when she describes her early days at the pottery:

"My first job was to make tea for everyone; I've never been completely happy in the kitchen and was pleased, as I am sure everyone else was, when I advanced to making handles at the sink instead of tea. It was at this sink that I learned to put handles on, until I reached a personal best of sixty an hour. Simple satisfaction was gained from the skill and discipline required and aesthetic pleasure from the rows of beautifully curved handles. Then, by means of a two step turn in this little room, I could sit down at the decorating table and become totally involved in the free design that was needed in the decorating of the larger 'raw' pots. I did a great deal of decorating while I was there as well as glazing and kiln packing".

Speed was all important at Briglin. Targets were always being set and passed, everyone was encouraged to compete with each other and themselves, but not at the expense of quality. Chris Jenkins remembers Brigitte demonstrating turning mugs quickly with the shavings hitting the wall ten feet away. The day's pots, barely leather hard, would be stacked high on the shelves of the Catterson Smith kiln ready to be fired the next day. Nothing was wasted, the shavings from turning, the rejected pieces were all recycled; the dry ones would be damped down until they were soft enough to be churned up in the pug machine.

In 1968 Alan Peascod, an Australian, spent a few months throwing and hand building at Briglin. He said recently, 'the attitudes towards production contributed towards my own ways of working later in life. I enjoyed the way 'raw' pots for bisque were packed into hot kilns, which helped me to realize that it was not important to slow the drying-down process in the hot Australian climate. It also encouraged me to explore fast firing methods, which I use even now. The scale of production was impressive, as were the decorating techniques. My time at Briglin helped in my appreciation of majolica and really good terracotta clay. When I am lecturing, I often speak about Briglin in 1968 and use the experience to advise on how important it is to ignore current beliefs and devise and develop one's own unique way of working".

The standard lines that had been started in Baker Street were carried on and others were added: mugs of all kinds and sizes, coffee pots, teapots, butter dishes, salt and pepper sets, goblets, ashtrays, storage jars, plates and bowls of all sizes and, always, the small and miniature animals and birds – some, money boxes, others just ornaments. The decoration changed gradually to include designs based on nature. Brigitte loved flowers and plants of all kinds, in autumn she used to get on her bicycle and go and collect leaves and copy the design direct from nature.

In addition to the long, standard runs a number of special pots were thrown and decorated. Mike Crosby-Jones describes, in greater detail than she has, how large vases, large decorative bowls and lamp bases were freely decorated by Lyn Colavecchia, many of them started while still leather hard or 'raw': "She used a hot wax made with three medium-sized candles to a third of a pint of paraffin. The different ways of decorating with wax resist are too numerous to describe fully: there is wax on 'raw' and wax on bisque, wax on 'raw' and sgraffittoed, then covered with an oxide on the banding wheel; there is painting the motif with wax on 'raw' then banding in the background; there is a combination of these two on 'raw' and a combination with further waxing on bisque. In fact every combination except wax on glaze. Decoration on earthenware is so much more important a part of the pot than on stoneware, because you don't get any help from the kiln, you get nothing for nothing, what you put in is what you get out". In the first ten years at Crawford Street, most of the oxide used was manganese, giving a brown or black colour. A few of the larger pots incorporated a cobalt and copper mix, giving an additional blue-green colouring.

As well as the standard runs and the larger pieces, commemorative and special order mugs and plates had always been an important part of Briglin's production. The plates, bowls and mugs decorated by Tony Barson for weddings, christenings and other special occasions went on for many years; he also decorated wall plates and bowls with scenes of London. Named mugs were a very popular line, although not always without problems. A huge order was received from a well-known public school. Dozens of mugs were duly produced, each hand painted with the name of the school. It was only when they were waiting to be packed, that someone asked, "Are you sure they spell it EATON?" For years after, tea and coffee in the pottery and in the homes of family and friends was drunk from mugs labelled EATON. Mike Crosby-Jones recalls, "an order from an advertising agency for one mug. One red mug. They would not disclose what it was for but were prepared to pay £100 for it. I remember thinking money for old rope, but not so. They rejected mug after mug until the thing they paid for was dead boring and would have been far better cast. The rest is history - the Nescafé mug is still running."

Brigitte's ability to get publicity was prodigious. She went to trade fairs exhibitions, festivals, both here and abroad, where she showed a range of pots and gave demonstrations; she sent out press releases and gave innumerable interviews to journalists. Her personal charm and vitality were often remarked upon, but the articles in the end were publicity for Briglin Pottery. Her association with Herbert Lom, who had become a director of the firm, brought theatre people to the shop, which, in itself, gave it publicity and many photo opportunities for journalists. She even appeared in November 1964 on television in a programme called Pick the Winner. She was adjudged to be the potter with the greatest skill and dexterity and was declared the winner.

Herbert Lom, Brigitte and Peter Sellers.

Pots from the 1950s.

CHAPTER 4

CONTACT WITH THE CRAFTSMEN POTTERS ASSOCIATION

On July 25, 1956 there had been an unprecedented meeting of potters, that set in motion the formation of the Craftsmen Potters Association of Great Britain. Organized by Walter Lipton, Marketing Officer for the Rural Industries Bureau, the intention was to work towards the setting up of a co-operative group of studio potters, who could command a single Export Licence. This would get round the problem of Purchase Tax – the precursor to VAT – which was pushing up prices at home and bedevilling the ability of the independent post-war potter to earn a living. However, as the scheme was initiated by an organization limited to helping country workshops, neither Briglin nor any other town potter was invited.

By the end of the meeting the original commercial idea had developed into something much more interesting. A working party was set up, charged with finding ways and means that would enable potters to share their experiences and initiate projects, that would enhance the common good, without sacrificing identity or independence. By the following spring this very disparate group of people had managed to clarify their ideas without too much strife.

An inaugural meeting was called in London, at the headquarters of the Art Workers Guild in Queen's Square. Word had got round and the room was packed with eager potters from both town and country. The suggested framework was read out and on the whole, approved. The working party was voted in as a Provisional Council. Then an argumentative speaker claimed that forming an association of potters was impossible, they would never agree – he had tried and failed; anyway, as Bernard Leach would not join, how could it possibly succeed? His negative approach galvanised the meeting into feeling that the only way forward was to shake off the St Ives strait-jacket, which was taken for granted by Hay Hill and the few other highly selective exhibiting societies. Very few people at the meeting knew each other, but most had in common that they made anything other than oriental reduced stoneware favoured by the followers of Bernard Leach. Briglin and the Oxshott Pottery were typical of these deviants; Briglin with its colourfully decorated earthenware; the Oxshott Pottery, where Rosemary Wren and her mother Denise made individual salt-glazed pieces. Both, like many others, were soundly established and the time was obviously ripe for a wider recognition of this greater freedom of expression .

At the meeting Brigitte, with outspoken enthusiasm, gave Briglin's support, but pointed out that town potters had no one to represent them at the meetings of the Council. She nominated her partner, Eileen. This was the start of Eileen's long association with the CPA and its mouthpiece, *Ceramic Review*, of which she became co-editor with Emmanual Cooper in 1969.

A modest Travelling Exhibition of members' work was organised by a sub-committee and the very first display was at Briglin Pottery in Baker Street in August 1957; a further one was held there in June 1958. There were so few specialist exhibitions of ceramics that this was a ground-breaking event in itself, quite apart from the diversity of the exhibits. Most of the exhibitors had, like Brigitte, been ensnared by the fascination of pottery during their training at art school, so thought radically as artists rather than traditionally as potters. The exhibitions were favourably reviewed in the art press.

The next step, in 1958, was to give the Association a legal identity, as a non-profit-making Friendly Society, so that it could open a bank account and take subscriptions. This seemed straightforward but in fact meant reaching agreement on legally binding rules, that covered everything from the name, how they could define themselves, who should be members, whether there should be a termination clause, who was to be on the Council, who would choose the officers. Everyone had different ideas on what activities should be undertaken: some cared most about financial advantages, others cared passionately about ethical principles. Eventually most people were satisfied.

A Foundation Meeting was called at a hotel in Southampton Row and a satisfying number of people joined. One of the conditions of membership was that an applicant had to have a kiln and a workshop; this was to exclude teachers, who used their art school facilities to make the occasional exhibition piece. The Founder Members included Michael Cardew, who gave a rousing speech, Michael Casson and many other now well-known potters, who were just starting out in the 1950s. After the meeting the Council elected Rosemary Wren as their Chairman.

When David Canter became the secretary of the CPA in 1960, his most important task was to find out whether it would be possible to finance and run its own premises. It seemed a wild dream, but at a meeting at Eileen's house in Regent's Park, he said that he had not only found a suitable situation – in Lowndes Court, off the then unknown Carnaby Street – but had worked out how to finance it.

The premises consisted of a ground floor and basement. The ground floor was made into an attractive showroom and the basement was used for storage – each member being allocated the same amount of shelf space. Michael Casson's sister, Pan Henry, was appointed manager, a job she did with great efficiency and charm. The whole

Early majolica mugs.

Half glazed flower pot with over-glaze decoration. Oxide brushed, white glazed jars and coffee pot.

White glazed earthenware dish with cobalt oxide brushwork.

Manganese oxide decoration with wax resist decoration under white glaze.

venture proved highly successful and in 1966 David Canter decided that they needed larger premises. These he found round the corner in Marshall Street. In August 1967 a publicity committee was appointed, before the move was made, which consisted of Pan Henry, Michael Casson, Brigitte and Alan Wallwork. Their ambitious aim was to display a selection of the best work by the best potters in the country. By the time the Marshall Street shop finally opened in December 1967, the floor space had been whittled down, there was very little storage space and the rise of Carnaby Street meant that parking for the potters and customers had become a nightmare.

Ironically too, less than ten years after the foundation of the CPA, some members of the Council were once more reflecting the very judgemental ideas that they had once rejected. Electric kilns, electric wheels were despised and slip-casting was regarded with horror. The original uncritical attitude towards what members exhibited was gradually being modified and meetings of the Council became more and more like a battleground. Briglin was tolerated – although despised by some – because it was successful and had established useful contacts, such as Joshua Taylor in Cambridge, which staged a CPA exhibition. Others were not so lucky. At one Council meeting the participants were asked to reject the work of Stanislaus Reychan. There was some fairly inconclusive discussion and than David Canter stood up and said how much he disliked the work and felt that it should not be exhibited. Stanislaus Reychan got up and left the room. On another occasion Denise Wren's work was singled out for rejection. It seemed that positions were being taken and Brigitte, for one, was certainly not in favour of what was happening. Her interest was in co-operative exhibiting and selling, not in the politics of the pottery world.

At a Council meeting in July 1967 Alan Wallwork suggested that sculptural pottery, very popular in America, was gaining favour in many art schools and should be represented by the CPA. Considerable opposition was expressed, but, eventually, in November 1968, it was agreed that art schools should be invited to submit sculptural works, made by their students, for exhibitions at the CPA, with a prize for the best piece to be judged by Hans Coper. The entries flooded in, but instead of allowing all of them to go forward, there was a lot of behind the scenes selection and in the end only half the normal show space was made available. Lots of people came to see the exhibition in April 1969 and, although they sold little, they took as much money in entrance fees as they normally did in sales. At the next Council meeting it was announced they they would not be repeating the exercise.

When Brigitte heard this, she offered to have all the rejected work put on show at Briglin in Crawford Street. A number of potters, who went on to make reputations in ceramics, accepted: Francis Hewlitt, James Campbell, Beresford Pealing, Glyn Hugo,

Pauline Zelinski and a number of others. At the CPA, little sold, but the exhibition was well attended, impressive and demonstrated dramatically the difference between Brigitte's attitude towards her fellow potters and that of the CPA.

From then onwards the active involvement of Briglin in the CPA ceased. Brigitte was so occupied running her own pottery that she neither wanted nor needed the CPA. Eileen, as co-editor of *Ceramic Review* remained attached to the CPA for years, but was no longer actively involved in Briglin. In fact, by this time, Brigitte had made contact with many other potters and craftsmen and had offered them a retail outlet in London through her shop.

Manganese oxide decoration with wax resist and white glaze.

Manganese oxide decoration with wax resist border and white glaze.

CHAPTER 5

EXPANSION

By the middle of the 1960s the success of Briglin Pottery was making the cramped conditions in the basement of 22 Crawford Street a real problem. Brigitte's first solution was to move some of the decorating and glazing to her mother's house, Tyrrells, at Effingham in Surrey. In 1951 her mother had applied for and got planning permission to convert a workshop attached to her house into a pottery. She used it to make small ceramic animals. Now a garage was converted into a pottery and the workshop used as a storeroom.

Mrs Goldsmith was a striking and, initially rather daunting person, who had trained as a doctor in Germany, but once she came to this country in 1934, had never practised. She would invite the young potters who worked at Tyrrells to call her Lotte, but she was always known as Mrs G. Her daughter-in-law, Beatrice, who married Brigitte's older brother George, tells of her first encounter with her future mother-in-law. Young and fresh from America, she had been invited down to Tyrrells for tea. She was dressed in a smart, tight suit and high-heeled shoes. Mrs Goldsmith insisted on taking her out for a drive in the huge car that she drove at the time. While out, they developed a puncture. "You jack it up, while I get the spare tyre," she ordered. Beatrice not only was she totally unsuitably dressed to do any such thing, but had never changed a wheel in her life. Seeing her confusion Mrs Goldsmith swept her aside, jacked the car up, changed the wheel and off they went again. Many years later Brigitte wrote: "Women who have neither husbands nor dogs get more like their mothers, or, as is more usual do their utmost to avoid doing so. Accepting is the answer... and keep on laughing at oneself". Mother and daughter were, in many ways, very similar.

Brigitte's second solution to the over-crowding in 22 Crawford Street was to take a lease on the basement of 23 Crawford Street. Soon after the ground floor too became available and Brigitte got Bill Siddons the architect to convert it into a shop and gallery, which was opened by the actress Sylvia Syms in November 1966. It seems that, once again, Briglin's spelling had let them down. After she had declared the studio open Sylvia looked at the pot they had made to commemorate the event and saw that they had spelt her name wrongly. She picked the pot up and dropped it on the floor where it broke into many pieces. A replacement was made, which she has to this day on the mantlepiece in her sitting room.

In 1967 the first exhibition was held in the gallery at 23 Crawford Street. Rosemary Wren writes, "I was asked to share the opening exhibition with Eileen. Our work made an interesting contrast. Eileen's cool, precise, abstract constructions against my hand-built stoneware animals, quietly thinking their own thoughts. David and Jane Attenborough had asked me to make a lasting record of Jimmy, the Hoolock Gibbon, that they had cared for since he was a tiny orphan. It was the centre-piece of the exhibition. Sir David opened the exhibition and became a frequent visitor".

The second basement provided a much larger storage space and packing area. Later, a separate decorating room was created at the front, under the pavement. The disadvantage was that everything had to be carried up the stairs in 22, round the outside and down the stairs in 23. One wet evening Brigitte suddenly decided that this was ridiculous. She took a hammer and banged a small hole in the brick wall which separated the two basements. An hour later a narrow doorway had been knocked through by Alan Pett. It remained there for twenty five years.

Another change that Brigitte had made in 1965 was to appoint Patrick Bedward (always known as Pat) as studio manager. In the early days at Baker Street this role had been filled by Eileen. With the increase in the size of the team Brigitte was feeling the need for greater organization. Pat was a trained social worker, so his role was purely administrative. When he went for a heart operation in 1966, Mike Crosby-Jones was appointed for two months to take his place. When Pat returned Mike continued to be studio manager and Pat became general manager. Mike describes the problems of

David Attenborough.

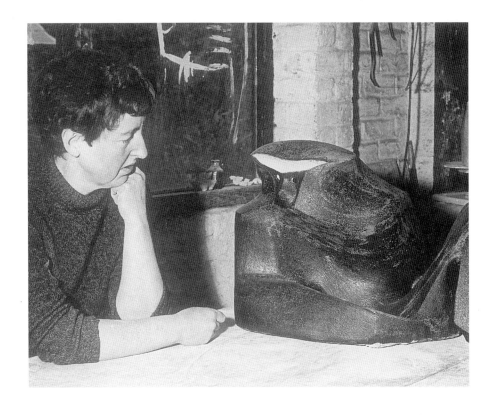

Rosemary Wren and some of her animals.

managing Briglin. "I used to work for eight or nine months and then go to Norway for three to write, usually in the winter. When I came back Brigitte wasn't very good at going back upstairs. I would offer an ultimatum and stomp off saying, "Call me when you've gone. I have to say that I was always nervous that they would manage quite well without me and was relieved when I got the call".

In addition to managers, Brigitte employed travellers to show the new lines to the contacts that she had already made and to find new ones. The packing and despatching of these pots became too much for Mr Houghton on his own so, in 1965, Brigitte took on Kitty Roche, the mother of one of her daughter Josephine's school friends, to look after the stockroom during the day. Kitty, like Mr Houghton, was loved by everyone and, like him, stayed at Briglin until the very end.

The pots that were being thrown during the 1960s and 70s are described by Alan Wallwork: "Briglin made subtle use of the characteristics of wheel-thrown ware. Although thrown against a straight edge, which gave a smooth exterior and made a variety of designs easier, the interior showed signs of the making process, the spiral throwing marks. The high firing softened the whiteness of the glaze, enhanced the throwing ridges and produced an interesting graininess from the red body, which showed through, while the unglazed body, on the base, darkened to near vitrification and minimal porosity".

At first the decorating at Tyrrells was done by Lyn Colavecchia, Priscilla Thoms and Margaret Tutt. They were later joined by others. Lyn tells how "Priscilla and I would travel down from Richmond, where we both lived. We would set off down the hill to catch a bus to Surbiton. There we would catch the train to Effingham Junction and then walk the country road to Tyrrells. We spent wonderful days potting in the shed, surrounded by apple trees, before reversing our journey, taking turns to push each other up the hill in Richmond, beside John Mills' house. In 1970 I went to America for a year, but on my return I went to live in one of the cottages at Tyrrells. Alan Pett and his wife Jane lived in the other cottage. We all seemed to have babies at the same time and continued to pot amongst domesticity, apples and country life".

One of Pat Bedward's jobs was to drive pots to and from Tyrrells. The studio there had two large Chromartie kilns to produce bisque as well as fire the decorated and glazed pots. In 1971 the original *daisy*, *scroll* and *willow* patterns were added to by one called *Tyrrells* which continued until 1973. Once a week Lyn would come up to London to decorate the larger pots, mostly vases, that were thrown in London and decorated 'raw'. Gradually greens and blues were added to the earthy browns of the 1950s and early 1960s and the early matt black and white was also re-introduced.

CHAPTER 6

TWENTY-FIRST BIRTHDAY PARTY
THE 1970s

On June 24th, 1969 the twenty-first anniversary of Briglin Pottery was celebrated with a party and an exhibition of Briglin Potters Past and Present. The full range of Briglin pots being made at the time was on show. In addition there were over four-hundred individual pieces by twenty-one potters. Brigitte took the opportunity to invite many of the people who had helped to build up and sustain the business over the years, to come back and exhibit their own work.

The potters represented were Brigitte herself; Eileen Lewenstein, the co-founder of Briglin; Adrian Abberly, a decorator, who originated the *scroll* design, the longest lasting of all the patterns; Daphne Ahlenius who, as Daphne Wells, had been so influential in the Baker Street days; Tony Barson, the artist whose humour and skill had added a range of mugs, plates and bowls; Tony Benham; Pat Birks, who had carried on the planters started in Baker Street; Rosalind Bliss, quality controller and decorator; Frances Benatt, thrower and turner; Tessa and Annette Fuchs, throwers, turners and decorators in Baker Street; Chris Jenkins, decorator, who started in the final year at Baker Street and worked for a short time in Crawford Street; Dan Killick, thrower; Jenny Miall Smith; Elizabeth McPhail, who was involved in the early days at Baker Street; Priscilla Thoms, decorator at Tyrrells; Sally Vinson, mainly glazer and decorator, both in Baker Street and Crawford Street; John Virando, the mainstay of the throwers in the 1960s; Alan Wallwork; Ann Wyn-Reeves, who worked for a short time in Baker Street and, with her husband, Ken Clark, remained a friend and adviser; and Max Zwissler, a potter from Switzerland, who worked in Baker Street.

Brigitte had always encouraged people to develop their own skills and this was very apparent in the pots shown in the exhibition, which included Eileen's abstract but firmly based constructions; stoneware flowers by Adrian Abberly; terracotta choir boys and mobiles by John Virando; birds and animals by Tessa Fuchs, Brigitte herself and Pat Birks; amusing tiles and plates by Tony Barson; hanging planters with a matt glaze by Sally Vinson; robust sculptural shapes by Chris Jenkins, including the saddle; and many other ornamental and functional things. The exhibition was given considerable coverage in the press and its appeal was increased by demonstrations of throwing and turning by Brigitte, both in London and Cambridge, where the exhibition moved to Joshua Taylor on July 25th.

THE TWENTY-FIRST BIRTHDAY
EXHIBITION

Mike Crosby-Jones gives a 'below-stairs' description of the party. "I always claim that it was Briglin that started the craze (appropriate word) for Raku. Up until Briglin's twenty-first birthday party, all potters had known about it, but no one had taken it seriously. We did Raku firing downstairs in the Catterson Smith. There were no elements in the door so we built a chamber inside the kiln, with refractory bats shielding the elements from the tongs. We added extra grog to the body, threw miniatures and cheated by firing them first. We plunged the hot pots into sawdust, then into water and had instant glazed pots. We used the standard zircon glaze with a tiny pinch of copper. I remember we smoked the party out, but among the notables present were Mick Casson, Rosemary Wren and Victor Margrie, who was head of pottery at Harrow College of Art – the most important college for pottery in the country. Mick Casson introduced Raku firing to Harrow as a consequence and Rosemary Wren fired a very impressive range of coil-built animals and birds for many years. No doubt some will tell you differently, but this is my version of events. Of course, Eileen was there and, being founder editor of *Ceramic Review*, gave the whole thing a good mention".

Parties were very much a feature of life at Briglin, as was hard work. At this time, in the late 1960s and early 1970s, they were turning out three-thousand pieces a week and took whole stands at the Birmingham and Blackpool Trade Fairs. They were also having a lot of fun. Brigitte never lost touch with her youth and loved to laugh and joke. Pam Butler writes: "You managed to create an atmosphere of such fun and creativity. Everyone loved working for you. Do you remember the day we all worked flat out and Alan and Jim threw three-hundred pots each and Irene and I pulled six-hundred handles?" There was always an element of surprise when working for Brigitte: she would take everyone on outings to visit other potters, to pick mushrooms, to picnic in Regent's Park, to swim in the Serpentine; on other days she would let everyone make what they wanted; often she went at six o'clock in the morning to Covent Garden and brought back boxes of cherries, plums, strawberries for everyone to enjoy. Always, when the weather allowed it, everyone would sit out on the pavement to drink coffee, have lunch or drink wine or beer at the end of the day.

The inflation of the late Sixties, which continued through the next decade, led Brigitte to think about other ways of making money apart from producing and selling pots. The cost of raw materials was rising and sales were being hit. She had always sold pots for other people and had also sold other things in the shop: jewellery, woven belts and scarves, glass and wood carvings; but now she wanted to find other ways of making money. The first thing she did, in 1969, was to rent the ground floor area of 23 Crawford Street to Alan Wallwork, who had a pottery in Dorset. They had been

Relaxing on the pavement.

friends for a long time and had many of the same customers. He stored and displayed his tiles, lamp bases and pots, which were sold and despatched with pots from Briglin. However, the parking in Crawford Street became progressively more difficult as did the driving in London. After less than a year he pulled out of his involvement with the small shop, but did continue to deliver pots and tiles to be sold through Briglin.

The ground floor of 23 Crawford Street then reverted to being used as a gallery, first being incorporated into the Briglin Potters Past and Present exhibition and later being used for special individual or group exhibitions. Rosemary Wren follows up the Raku story when she says, "Pottery looked good in the brick-floored, architect designed gallery and in November 1969 it was used for an exhibition of my "Hand-built animals in Raku", a technique which was still unusual, so a lot of potters came to see it". She goes on, "Later, in 1971, Briglin had an exhibition of Oxshott potters, with elephants made by my mother, Denise K. Wren, creatures made by my partner, Peter Crotty, my own animals and birds and a collection of work by Terry and Beverley Bell-Hughes". In May 1970 there was an exhibition of Ceramics by Tessa Fuchs, Adrian Abberley and Mary O'Flynn and in November 1970 Woven Textiles by Pat Holtom and Jewellery by Dafna Grant, Hamish Campbell and Lois Sachs. These were followed, throughout the Seventies, by a number of similar exhibitions, the cost of which were borne by the exhibitors.

Regulations on workshops, union disputes and rising prices were all making life

Making pinch pots in Gozo.

difficult for small businesses. Early in 1969 Alan Wallwork, Brigitte and Pat Bedward had begun discussing the possibility of setting up a workshop, where life was cheaper and the sun shone more often. They had two contacts in Gozo, the small island off Malta: Barbara Huxley, a graphic artist and Pat Holtom, who had set up a weaving studio there and was already sending things back to sell in the Briglin shop. Brigitte and Pat Bedward went out there in the autumn of 1969 to explore the possibilities. They came back with lots of photographs of ruins that were for sale – one of which Brigitte had bought.

She never set up a pottery out there, but she did have a memorable pottery party, described by Alan:

"In 1970, as soon as Brigitte's ruin had been made roughly habitable, she was inviting people to stay there. I have photos of Brigitte, her daughter Jo, Tony Barson and his two girls, Susie and Morag, my then wife, Liz, and our children, Amanda, Dillon and Tristan. Everybody is sitting in the courtyard making pinch pots. I had discovered that some great mounds of what looked like clay, out on the sun-baked hillside near Brigitte's house, were indeed clay, that could be made workable by the addition of beach sand from Ramla. In a clearing in the jungle of prickly pear that then filled Brigitte's walled garden, I started to build a Raku kiln, with the many blocks of squared-off limestone that lay around.

"In that climate the pots soon became bone dry and Brigitte, with her customary optimism, invited people from far and wide to come to a kiln-firing party that evening.

All I had to fire the kiln with were the masses of dry, prickly pear fronds, that littered the ground. I knew they would burn fiercely, too fiercely it turned out, as only about a quarter of the pots survived the firing. Those that did looked nice. After the firing was done Brigitte produced a big pan of fish which she cooked on the fire-box of the kiln for everybody to enjoy".

The other possible move from the centre of London that Alan Wallwork, Pat Bedward and Brigitte discussed, was to a small factory in Mortlake, which would be far more convenient for travelling to and from Effingham and for Alan to deliver to and from Dorset. Brigitte went so far as to throw a party in a house that was for sale, to see if she liked it.

However, Brigitte's enthusiasm for new ideas was often misleading and she never fully intended to move from Crawford Street. As Alan writes, "I at last grasped that Briglin was very far from being the coldly efficient money-making machine that some potters thought it was and despised it for being. I had been trying to suggest ways that seemed to me would make it more efficient, but I was missing the point. The position in Crawford Street with all the problems of access, the small underground workshops, the cramped storage space was only part of the story. It was the village atmosphere of Crawford Street, the passing, often exotic, clientele, the people who dropped in for a chat, the posh greengrocer opposite, a splendid ironmonger off to one side, Jimmy the antique dealer, David Shilling's hat shop on the corner, Mrs Worthington dispensing gin in the off-licence and many, many other amenities that Brigitte loved. Also the workers at Briglin were not just the necessary labour force to keep the pots being produced, they were all Brigitte's extended family and the centre of London could provide an endless supply of young people wanting to join the family".

Although Brigitte did not set up a pottery in Gozo, she was very drawn to the place and to her house, which she named Fort Appleby – probably, in a hundred or two-hundred years time, people will wonder who General Appleby was and how he contributed to the defence of the island! In 1972 she decided that she would go there for a few months and leave Pat Bedward in charge of the pottery. He had been involved with it for six years and she felt confident that he could run it while she was away.

He had always thought it could be more efficient, so, when he was given a free hand, he tried to make a number of changes. He wanted everyone to clock-in and asked them all to give a job description and define their responsibilities. As a great many of the people who came to Briglin were totally, or almost totally, inexperienced, this was not very practical. Typical of these was Pam Butler, who joined the team at the end of 1971 and worked there for six years. She had walked into the shop, asked about the pottery and was told to go downstairs and talk to Brigitte. When she got to

Sunflower pattern.

the basement Brigitte asked her if she could make tea. When she said yes, she was shown where the kettle was and before she knew where she was she was employed. To begin with she made tea and did other menial jobs, but gradually she learnt how to pack a kiln, make handles and eventually decorate. Although Brigitte did not explicitly subscribe to the Leach philosophy, she certainly believed in team work, co-operative interest and, most of all, she thought people should enjoy what they were doing. However bossy and difficult she could be, she always gave her workers a big hug at the end of the day. Suddenly all this had changed. The warmth, the flexibility, the enthusiasm had gone and been replaced by systems.

When Brigitte came back from Gozo, she found a very unhappy workforce and a business in financial trouble. After the initial shock and distress that someone she had trusted had let her down, she set too, with renewed energy, to rebuild the business herself. The first thing she did was to reduce the number of items on the wholesale list from seventy-six to fifty-eight – cutting out the things that did not sell so well. She changed the clay that they used, cutting out the grog to make the wax resist decoration easier to apply. She also introduced a new pattern called *sunflower*, to add to the ones which were being produced which were *scroll* and *Tyrrells*. New designs at Briglin often evolved from a co-operative effort. Brigitte encouraged everyone to throw out ideas which were then worked on. These ideas often originated from the one-off pots, which were decorated 'raw'. In 1973 Pam Jenkins took a design that Lyn Colavecchia had put on to a lamp base, some while before, changed it slightly and it became *fern*. In 1974 *Tyrrells* was replaced by *twist*.

In 1974 Briglin was flourishing again. Fifteen potters were working full-time and once more producing three to four-thousand pieces a week. The London team consisted of Jim Johnson and Alan Pett, throwers; Stephen Russell, turner, Pam Jenkins, decorator and other less experienced workers; Lyn and Lynette were decorating at Effingham, where a certain amount of bisque was also being produced. In the Evening Standard of April 3 there was an article entitled *Wheel of fortune turns for potters*, in which Brigitte told Stephanie Thompson that "thousands of shoppers drop in to buy – a large percentage of them tourists – and, on the wholesale side, buyers come from as far afield as Japan, America, Canada and Germany". She went on, "Britain is now becoming a major centre for young students and even accomplished potters. At our studio we have dozens of applications from potters from all over the world. There is hardly a country we haven't had an application from". The article was

The designs in 1974.

illustrated with two photos, one showing Pam Butler working alongside a young potter from Japan.

Brigitte was feeling so enthusiastic about things by the middle of 1974 that she suddenly decided to give a party at Tyrrells. Masses of strange shaped pinch goblets, which could double as candlesticks, were made in London and Effingham; Mike Lovitt and Alan Pett were instructed to build a barbecue and were made responsible for cooking large quantities of hot dogs; lots of drink was imported and about seventy to eighty people came. Amongst them was a detective from Paddington Green Police Station, whom Brigitte had got to know; he brought with him a police jazz band, who played extremely loudly long into the night. When the local police from Effingham arrived, after an irate neighbour had complained of the noise, they were introduced to the detective and joined in the fun, reporting back to the station that they had been unable to trace the source of the noise.

Brigitte's connection with the theatre and film world involved her in some unusual as well as lucrative ventures. The designers of a television play starring John Thaw asked if they might come to Briglin to see what a pottery looked like. The play was about a potter, John Thaw, who murdered his wife, incinerated her in his kiln and then used the ashes to make a glaze! The producers asked if she could let them have a male potter, whose hands could be shown making a pot, which John Thaw could then finish. Brigitte and Alan Wallwork went along to the studio and Alan made a coil pot

The Generation Game.

leaving John Thaw to add a piece to the top. In 1979, Brigitte herself appeared on television in the Generation Game, making a large elephant with huge floppy ears.

By 1977 Briglin was the only studio pottery still manufacturing in the west end of London. The Three Day Week, the oil crisis in the Middle East and ever increasing inflation had made life very uncertain for small businesses. But Brigitte's philosophy of hiring young, inexperienced people and teaching them, meant that she could keep her wage bill relatively low. Typical of the people, who came to work for Briglin, was Tony Clarke. He heard an advertisement on Capital Radio, went for an interview and was immediately offered a job. He was nineteen when he joined the team in 1976 and two years later, having learnt the rudiments at Briglin, went to Harrow College of Art, where he was taught by Dan Killick, a former Briglin pottery. When, in 1977, Alan Pett left to set up a studio at Harefield and Lyn left to set up a studio in Lincolnshire, everything was moved to London. With all the decorating back in Crawford Street, Brigitte changed the patterns in 1977 and again in 1978, *scroll* remaining as the only design not based on nature. It was to be the most long-lasting of all the designs, partly because it was popular, but also because it was a good one for inexperienced decorators to start on. In 1977 the patterns were: *fern, honeysuckle, scroll, sunflower* and *thistle*. *Honeysuckle* was developed by Brigitte and Lynette Preedy using a Japanese brush, which gave it a special oriental quality. In 1978 *fern* was dropped and *water lily* and *autumn* were introduced. The following year *willow* was added.

In April 1978 Brigitte realized a long held ambition to visit China. Organized by the CPA, the aim of the visit was to see the country and its people as they live, work and make pottery and to experience something of its history through buildings and museum collections. An application for a cultural group with special interest in pottery was sent to Luxingshe (China Travel Service) and, after some negotiation, the journey was confirmed. They would enter China from Hong Kong, travel northwards via Canton, Kweilin, Changsha and Sian and spend the last five days in Peking. The whole visit would last seventeen days.

The twenty-four members of the group included Eileen Lewenstein. As they crossed the border from Hong Kong into China at the Shum Chum Railway Station, they were a little disconcerted to find that they were officially known as 'British Ceramics'. It took them a long time to convince their official guides – Mr Feng and Mr Chin – that they wanted to see hand made pots. Peter Dick wrote in the Ceramic Review: "The official policy seems to be that foreign visitors should be shown the most modern factories... Other groups seem to have been perfectly happy with this, but British Ceramics were not. In houses, shops and on the verges of roads we were constantly seeing vigorous pottery for everyday use: rice bowls jolleyed and hand decorated; thrown plant pots and pickle jars and huge store jars with rich tenmoku glazes. We wanted to see these pots being made, but the reaction of our hosts was first that they were of little importance and then, when pushed, that for various reasons it was impossible to reach that particular factory".

The most interesting pottery – or factory, as they were all called – that they saw was at Tung Kwan, where they have been making pots for over two-thousand years. As they drove into the town, kilns, including a dragon kiln, could be seen climbing up every hillside and the houses were built with discarded jars. They saw huge store jars being made by two methods. The first used a mixture of the hand-based techniques of slabbing, press moulding and coiling, with a final modification by paddle and anvil. In the second method the jars were formed by large scale jolleying in a cloth lined wooden mould and then, similarly, brought to shape by paddle and anvil.

Although sometimes frustrated while they were there, when the group arrived back in England they found that they had learnt a lot from their visit: glazing the outside of a shallow dish using hollow bamboo as a suction pad; reducing glaze absorption by coating the surface of the pot with ball clay slip; glazing the inside of plates and bowls by securing them on a wheelhead, pouring a little glaze into the centre, then spinning the wheel fast, spreading the glaze evenly by centrifugal force; using fabric moulding instead of paper for lining; making a turning tool by cutting it from very wide bamboo with chisel shaped ends and a thin flexible middle; making a tapered rather than straight hole cutter, which never becomes blocked.

Brigitte came back full of enthusiasm for everything: the cleanliness of the towns, the friendliness of the people and the marvellous food they had been given. She immediately made a charcoal cooking stove – the Chinese equivalent of a barbecue – out of heavily grogged stoneware clay and cooked a Chinese meal in a wok on the balcony of her flat in London. She also mounted a photographic exhibition of the visit at 22 and 23 Crawford Street in December 1978. In an interview for the Marylebone Mercury, she said, "Even the litter bins in a street in Kweilin were works of art in blue, green and white glazed pottery". Perhaps it was the memory of these, or the wealth of archeological and historical pots that she saw in museums throughout China, that influenced her decoration in the Eighties.

CHAPTER 7

THE LAST TEN YEARS

Briglin in the Eighties belonged mainly to three people: Brigitte, Alan Pett and Diane Ibanez. Diane starts the story, "I returned to London in 1980 and, on one of my trips to the West End, decided to visit my old friend Brigitte. I walked in the door of 22 Crawford Street, got a big smile and a huge hug. There was no "How are you?", "When did you arrive?", "How long are you staying?", just "Have you come for the shop?" It turned out that she wanted to start to take things a little easier, cut down on staff, production and responsibilities and so had no further use for the second part of the shop. I tried to explain that I hadn't thought of having a business in London, wouldn't know what type of business to have. All this fell on deaf ears. "But darling, wouldn't it be wonderful to have you next door. There must be something you can do."

Brigitte and Diane had met many years before in the Sixties. Diane was working in the Canary Islands as a representative for a travel company in Tenerife: "On one transfer day, which I expected to be the same as any other, I went to the airport, picked up my new group, unaware that a passenger on the coach would change a part of my life. Brigitte was there with her daughter Josephine. If you have met her you will know what I mean when I say that things are never quite the same again. I took all the passengers to their hotels and thought that was that. A few days later who should come into my Art Gallery but a very surprised Brigitte. "What are you doing here?" You're supposed to be looking after tourists". I explained that this was my husband's gallery, where we sold his pictures and my hand-painted clothes, when I wasn't ferrying around coach loads of tourists. She was thrilled that she could meet a local Spanish artist and she bought one of his paintings. She told me she was a potter, had a shop in London and the next thing I know I'm an agent for Briglin Pottery in Spain and the Canary Islands and am selling it in my shop in Puerto de la Cruz. In 1970 this came to an end when I moved to Lanzarote". Ten years later she was in London.

She continues the story: "There was something I could do. I had a friend who had the Newgate Gallery in the City and I asked him if he would be interested in my running Newgate Gallery II. He agreed to give it a try, so half of Briglin became a Gallery and picture framer. After a couple of years I found my interest waning and started looking for a new idea. I discussed it with Brigitte and she said, "Why don't we open a plant shop together?" She had always had a selection of plants to display in her pots. "I'll sell the pots, you take care of the plants. Maybe we could sell cut flowers as well". And so Windowbox was born. We redecorated the shop, went to Covent Garden, filled the place with plants and flowers and sat back and waited".

Windowbox was a great success. They sold huge indoor plants and seasonal flowers. Brigitte planted hanging baskets and windowboxes and she and Diane took it in turns to go to the market at five in the morning. It was partly her involvement in this new venture that made Brigitte decide, in 1982, to stop throwing and firing in Crawford Street. Although the seventies, after the crisis in 1972, had been a successful time for Briglin pots, things were getting more and more difficult, especially in the middle of London. Also, for some time, Brigitte had been suffering from a back problem, which made sitting at a wheel extremely painful. She had always farmed out a certain amount of throwing and firing to other potters – people who had trained or worked at Briglin and gone off to start their own studios. When Brigitte gave away the wheel that remained and dismantled the kilns, she continued to decorate, but depended on Alan Pett to throw and fire pots for her.

Alan had started working for Briglin in August 1966. He was sixteen and had come straight from Bourne Secondary Modern School in Ruislip. He had not had an easy time at school as he is dyslexic – not something that was well understood at that time. However, there were two teachers who had a great influence on his life: John Phillips ran the pottery and sculpture department and introduced him to clay and the work of contemporary potters; Alan Herman ran the woodwork department and encouraged all Alan's artistic abilities. Before he left school he went for two interviews: one at Briglin and the other at sign-writers. He took the Briglin job because it offered slightly more money.

He is remembered, by those who worked with him, as mischievous, great fun and very hard working. In 1969 Brigitte encouraged him to go for two years to Harrow College of Art, the foremost college for pottery in the country. In 1972 Alan was back at Briglin and, in the Spring of 1973, went, with his new wife, to live in one of the cottages at Tyrrells. At that time Mrs Goldsmith was looking after the shop in Crawford Street and Alan used to drive her up and down most days with pots and her dog Toby. She always had dogs – little ones with fairly unpleasant characters – she even brought one into the country, smuggled under her mink coat, when she came from Germany in 1934. Both she and Toby added colour to the pottery and are remembered by all who worked there at the time and, almost surely, by many of the customers who came to the shop. Toby would take no notice of anyone except his owner and would treat chair legs, table legs and even men's legs as though they were trees or lamp-posts.

In 1977 after four years of hard work and fairly idyllic living, Alan, once more encouraged by Brigitte, decided to set up his own studio in Harefield. She never tried to hang on to the people who worked for her, but she rarely lost touch with them. In 1982 after Alan had helped her to dismantle the kiln and get rid of the wheel that remained in Crawford Street, she received an order from an old customer, who ran a hotel in the Seychelles. Reluctant to turn it down, she asked Alan if he would like to take it on. He agreed to do it and Brigitte went down to Harefield to help with the decorating. She found that she enjoyed this so much that it became a regular event. Most of the throwing was done by Alan, but she would go down almost every week to decorate. She would arrive with baskets of fruit and food she had cooked. Brigitte had never liked making plates but Alan was expert at it. One of his most popular lines was name-plaques for houses, which required much the same skill as making plates. He threw and Brigitte decorated two whole sets of plates of two sizes, dishes, bowls of various sizes, mugs and goblets. One was decorated in green and shipped out to the house in Kitzbuhel, that had been left by her aunt Hilde to Brigitte and her cousin; the other was decorated with a blue chrysanthemum pattern and was sold. Often she would arrive for dinner with friends bearing a bowl, full of some delicious pudding she had made, and leave the bowl as a present. People going to dinner with her would sometimes find their places marked with named mugs. Her decorations at this time were all from nature: fruit and flowers of all kinds painted in green and blue and brown, onto white, tin-glazed stoneware.

As well as decorating pots, running the shop and helping with Windowbox, she took up painting again, something she had not done for many years. She chose to use

Windowbox.

Wax decoration allows the red earthenware to contrast with the white glaze.

Crafted features with manganese oxide, white glazed.

Incised designs carried out on the 'leather hard' pot.

Simple striped pot, incised decoration
and wax resist.

Bottles with combed sgraffito through manganese
oxide.

Scroll, the longest lasting design, wax resist and manganese oxide decoration.

Delicate brushwork with some wax and sgraffito on the vase.

Tall bottle, sgraffito through banded wax, cobalt oxide, white glazed. Flagon, incised linear decoration.

Vases, sgraffito work through wax then coloured with cobalt oxide, white glazed. Jug painted copper oxide, white glazed.

White tin glazed stoneware decorated with strong, confident brushwork in cobalt oxide.

White tin glazed stoneware with copper oxide brushwork.

pastels, possibly because, like decorating earthenware, the end result is exactly the same as the application: the colours do not change nor does the texture. Many of the things she painted were pots and flowers – favourite pots made by other people, some filled with flowers. Her pictures sold in the shop and, in 1989, were exhibited at the Gallery Upstairs in Henley in Arden.

This exhibition was shared with Guy Taplin. Brigitte met Guy in the early Eighties, while they were both queuing for icecreams in Regent's Park. He was at the time Keeper of Birds and also carved wooden birds. When Brigitte heard about this she offered to sell them in her shop. They were immediately popular and he soon stopped working in Regent's Park and became a full time sculptor. Since then he has continued to be very successful and his birds sell for considerable prices.

The shop continued to flourish. It had never been just a retail showroom for Briglin pots, always a treasure house for anything that took Brigitte's fancy: other people's pots, woodcarvings, glass, fabrics, rugs, toys, jewellery. Some things were costly, others cost little – the perfect place to buy presents. Diane Ibanez said of it, "Briglin was a unique shop that sold creative beautiful things, always full of happy, chatting people. It was a place with a lot of soul".

However, when the lease of 23 Crawford Street came up for renewal and Alan Pett told her he was planning to move to Scotland, she decided to call it a day. In 1990, the lease on 22 Crawford Street was sold. She threw a party and soon after, with considerable sadness, closed the door for the last time. But Brigitte never remained sad for long. By this time Josephine, married to Michael Bor, was soon to produce her first son and Brigitte was preparing to launch herself into being a grandmother with the same energy and enthusiasm that she had put into starting the pottery forty-two years earlier.

Rosemary Wren wrote recently, "It is sad but inevitable that Briglin Pottery no longer exists – inevitable because its designs and working techniques could only have been thought up by those two particular people at that particular time. Many small pottery workshops were set up in the 1950s but very few in London itself. Carnaby Street had been devoted to skilled and small-scale craftsmen, but by the time the Craftsmen Potters Shop was set up they had nearly all vanished; town planning and the every increasing health and safety provisions of the Factory Acts made their continued existence impossible. I suspect that anyone hoping to set up a pottery today in the subterranean labyrinths of Baker Street would find their path blocked". Mike Crosby Jones adds, "Today there are no workshops like Briglin and, as a consequence, subsequent generations of potters have been obliged to become artists, as there is nowhere left for them really to learn the craft. Most have become 'one-off' merchants, as to make two pots alike would pose too much of a problem".

The closing party.

Alan Frewin, who worked at Briglin from 1966 to 1969 wrote to Brigitte in 1999: "You say that Briglin seems a little like history, well it is history and not only yours but the history of all the people whose lives you have touched. When you created Briglin you started a lot more than a pottery, more a kind of catalyst.

I know that not all your memories are necessarily happy ones, or perhaps you feel sad because it is in the past. However, I do know that all the people who I still have contact with, think of you and their time at Briglin with very great affection. That's something to feel very good about". She did.

In the month that Brigitte died – April 2000 – an article was published in *Antiques Info* called *A New Series on Craft Pottery – Briglin*. The article is written by Graham Gower and, after an introductory few paragraphs about the early history of the pottery he says, "Although the name Briglin is well known and respected among students of ceramic art, it has yet to find a broader appreciation among collectors and dealers. However, with the rising interest in collecting craft pottery in general, it comes as no surprise to note that pieces carrying the Briglin mark are now attracting serious attention and are fast becoming sought after as collectors items". He then describes the pottery that was produced and lists a number of items that have been bought by collectors. He ends: "The closing of the pottery passed almost unnoticed but the legacy of Briglin is still with us. In the long history of the pottery many aspiring young potters came to work at Briglin, learning or practising their skills before moving on to become renowned potters in their own right. For the collector the legacy is quality pottery that is worth collecting in a market that is just beginning to recognise the ceramic work of Brigitte Appleby and Eileen Lewenstein".

OBITUARY OF BRIGITTE APPLEBY IN THE INDEPENDENT 19 APRIL, 2000

For over 40 years Brigitte Appleby ran Briglin Pottery in Crawford Street, London, just off Baker Street, training large numbers of potters, many of whom went on to set up their own studios, and combining commercial acumen with discriminating taste. Briglin pots were regularly shown in exhibitions and featured in books on the decorative and applied arts, but the strength of Briglin was not so much in exhibition pieces but in sound, practical, attractive pots for daily use.

She was born Brigitte Goldschmidt into a wealthy and close-knit family in Leipzig, the middle child of three, with one older brother, George, and one younger, Rainer, both of whom she adored. With ominous moves against Jews in Germany the family moved to England in 1934, settling in a large, luxurious, pseudo-Elizabethan house in Osxhott, Surrey, which her father generously threw open as a staging post for the flood of refugees that followed.

Keen to receive what she called a proper education, Brigitte became a pupil at Guildford High School, where she declared she wanted to do something worthwhile and considered nursing. The headmistress refused to provide a reference, on the basis that Brigitte did not stick at anything – an unfair assessment that rankled throughout her life.

Inspired by her Aunt Hilda, who was a painter, Brigitte Goldschmidt became a student at the Central School of Arts and Crafts in London, studying painting, drawing and ceramics. In the pottery studio she was introduced to the craft by Gilbert Harding-Green, and was immediately bitten by the clay bug. Putting her desire to do something practical and worthwhile into practice she went to work for Donald Mills, who ran a pottery in Borough.

Here she met the potter Eileen Lewenstein, a lifelong friendship was struck and in 1948 they joined forces to set up Briglin – a combination of their Christian names – that would produce well-designed functional pots in earthenware with a rich white glaze and simple painted decoration. The pots had more in keeping with the simplicity and strength of Scandinavian wares than the more sombre Leach-inspired pots then in vogue.

Goldschmidt and Lewenstein were part of the renaissance of craft in the post-war period, and with a mixture of artistic and ideological zeal produced pots at affordable prices. Like its near neighbours Lucie Rie and Hans Coper, two other émigré potters, Briglin placed itself firmly within the modern movement, dealing with function, truth to materials and the role of the well-designed object within the home. Against the odds the pottery survived by selling low-priced pieces in central London.

A brief marriage in 1950 to Stephen Appleby, an aero-engineer notable for his earlier exploits with the Flying Flea, survived for a year or two. A long, happy partnership with the actor Herbert Lom followed, with whom Brigitte had a daughter, Josephine. In 1959 Eileen Lewenstein left to set up her own studio and Appleby became sole owner, extending the premises and running a team of about ten potters, producing literally thousands of pots and shipping them round Britain.

Keenly supportive of the burgeoning craft pottery movement, Brigitte Appleby was one of the founding members of the Craftsmen Potters Association, and served for many years on its council. She and others helped to put it on a sound financial footing to ensure its survival, helped it acquire shop premises in a then forgotten quarter of Soho and was one of a stream of volunteers helping to run it. She encouraged young potters, supported the fresh and innovative rather than the conventional, and above all was committed to making the co-operative enterprise succeed.

The survival of Briglin, its ability to change and adapt, was clear proof that Appleby could stick at something in which she believed. At one point part of the ground floor was converted into an attractive shop selling pots by other potters. Here Appleby could be ruthless in rejecting work she thought not up to standard, but equally generous in making you a gift of an admired pot. In 1990 the pottery finally closed. Rents were rising and the market changing, but with energy undimmed Appleby moved on to other projects, including returning to her early love of painting. It was typical of Appleby's generosity and enthusiasm for the craft that some of her favourite subjects were pots made by other potters.

I met Brigitte Appleby for the first time when I was a young hopeful looking for a job as a potter at Briglin in the early 1960s. Brigitte, a vivacious, enthusiastic, bouncy, smiling woman, showed me round the cramped but well-ordered studio in what seemed like a warren of rooms, and asked knowingly whether I could throw. Behind us the team of skilled potters effortlessly made a variety of forms that included mugs, coffee-pots, plates and vases.

Before I had chance to reply she quickly said that the pottery had no vacancies, but urged me not to be discouraged and to look for training elsewhere. The generosity, the friendliness and the welcome seemed to come easily and despite having numerous tasks waiting to be attended in this busy, flourishing workshop, Brigitte was helpful in offering constructive advice.

EMMANUAL COOPER

Brigitte Miriam Clare Goldschmidt, potter: born Leipzig, Germany 13 September 1926; married 1950 Stephen Appleby (marriage dissolved), (one daughter by Herbert Lom); died Egginton, Derbyshire 12 April 2000.

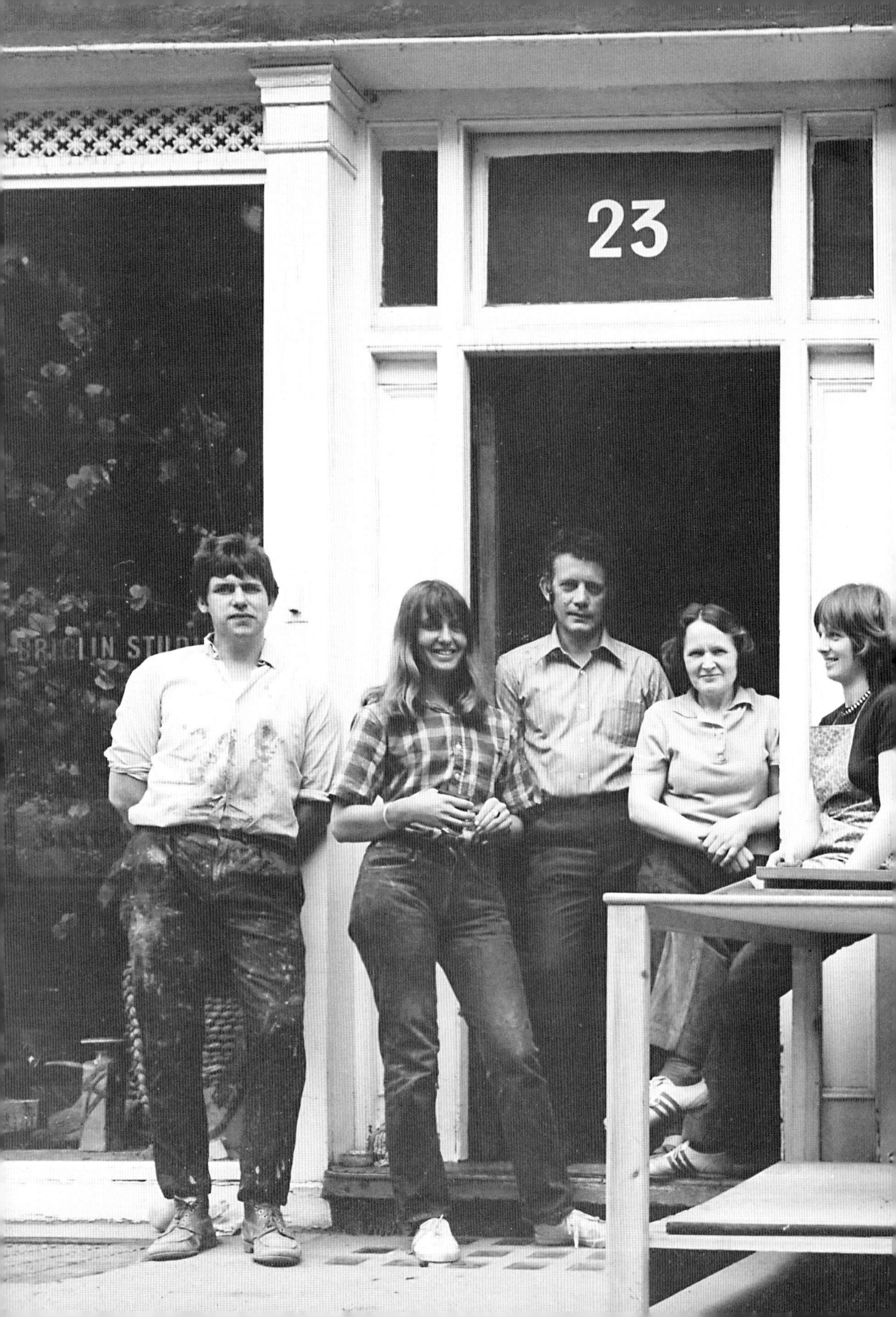
23